HAL•LEONARD
INSTRUMENTAL PLAY-ALONG

AUDIO
ACCESS
INCLUDED

FLUTE

JAMES BOND

PLAYBACK+
Speed • Pitch • Balance • Loop

To access audio visit:
www.halleonard.com/mylibrary

Enter Code
8327-6761-6718-0425

Audio arrangements by Peter Deneff

ISBN 978-1-4950-6078-6

Music Sales America

EXCLUSIVELY DISTRIBUTED BY

HAL•LEONARD®
7777 W. BLUEMOUND RD. P.O. BOX 13819 MILWAUKEE, WI 53213

Visit Hal Leonard Online at
www.halleonard.com

DIAMONDS ARE FOREVER

from DIAMONDS ARE FOREVER

Words by DON BLACK
Music by JOHN BARRY

Flute

FOR YOUR EYES ONLY

from FOR YOUR EYES ONLY

Flute

Lyrics by MICHAEL LESSON
Music by BILL CONTI

FROM RUSSIA WITH LOVE

from FROM RUSSIA WITH LOVE

Flute

Words and Music by
LIONEL BART

Moderate Ballad

GOLDFINGER

from GOLDFINGER

Flute

Music by JOHN BARRY
Lyrics by LESLIE BRICUSSE and ANTHONY NEWLEY

JAMES BOND THEME

FLUTE

By MONTY NORMAN

LIVE AND LET DIE

from LIVE AND LET DIE

Flute

Words and Music by PAUL McCARTNEY
and LINDA McCARTNEY

NOBODY DOES IT BETTER

from THE SPY WHO LOVED ME

Music by MARVIN HAMLISCH
Lyrics by CAROLE BAYER SAGER

FLUTE

ON HER MAJESTY'S SECRET SERVICE - THEME

FLUTE

By JOHN BARRY

SKYFALL

from the Motion Picture SKYFALL

FLUTE

Words and Music by ADELE ADKINS
and PAUL EPWORTH

A VIEW TO A KILL

from A VIEW TO A KILL

Flute

Words and Music by JOHN BARRY
and DURAN DURAN

WRITING'S ON THE WALL

from the film SPECTRE

Flute

Words and Music by SAM SMITH
and JAMES NAPIER

YOU ONLY LIVE TWICE

from YOU ONLY LIVE TWICE

Flute

Music by JOHN BARRY
Lyrics by LESLIE BRICUSSE